THE BEAUTY OF NEW ZEALAND'S
SOUTH ISLAND

THE BEAUTY OF NEW ZEALAND'S

SOUTH ISLAND

WARREN JACOBS
Text by
Errol Brathwaite

Kowhai Publishing Ltd

Key to location of plates

Endpaper: Morning Light, Head of Lake Wakatipu
Page 2-3: Kaiteriteri Coast
Page 4: Rock and Pilar Range near Sutton, Otago

CONTENTS

THE SOUTHERN ALPS.

A first-time visitor to New Zealand, describing his impressions, might well say, simply, "The country is mountainous." It wouldn't be telling the full tale, but such a description would convey a fairly adequate picture. New Zealand *is* mountainous; and even in those areas where it is not, its plains, coastlines, lakes, cities, rolling pastoral landscapes are brooded over, dominated by mountains. Wherever the eye looks inland, it is guided on and upwards to a high, serrated skyline, sometimes dark with forest to the crests of its notched ridges, sometimes dazzling with year-round snow. Single summits, or prides of powerful peaks, mountains are the predominant feature, the landscape rampant, the key component which establishes the character of the entire scene.

This, in varying degrees, is true of both North and South Islands. But it is in the South Island that the mountains reach a perfection of grandeur. The South Island is more spectacularly creased than the North Island. Viewed from almost any internal airline flight, vast areas of it are seen to be as crumpled as a discarded piece of paper, with range upon range of titanic pressure-fold ridges, dovetailed or massively tangled chains of peaks, stretching away for as far as the eye can see.

The Tasman Mountains, the Richmond Range, the St. Arnaud and Spenser Mountains and the Kaikoura Ranges fan out northward from the great rugged chain and uprising forested spurs which rise up to form the Southern Alps; and the Southern Alps, at their southern end, fray out into a wild and well-nigh impenetrable tangle and knotting of mountains covering perhaps half of the Otago-Southland region.

The Southern Alps, of course, take pride of place. They are the show-piece, the magnificent spectacle, that attracts visitors in their awed thousands. In their folds and in the pleatings of their skirts they hold lakes of unrivalled splendour. On their valley-riven flanks, between their massive lateral arms, they cradle splendid glaciers. In this massif alone there are more than a hundred and thirty peaks that rise over 2,400 metres, chief of which is *Aorangi*, the Cloud Piercer, officially and prosaically named Mount Cook by official and prosaic Captain Stokes of H.M.S. *Acheron*, after the great 18th century navigator.

It is the mountains, of course, that order the country's climate. The South Island is exactly what its name describes, a southern ocean island, with an island's capricious weather patterns. That is to be expected. What is astonishing, however, is the number of climatic variations, distinct climatic zones, within such a small compass; for the island is a mere 750km long by 250km wide at its widest point. And that — by continental terms — is a small area in which to have, side-by-side, zones which are temperate in climate, with a moderate to low rainfall, areas which are dry to the point of being

Snowfall, Craigieburn Range, Canterbury.

The Cragieburn Range, high above Lake Lyndon on the road to Arthurs Pass, is a drab area in summer, more like a gigantic gravel heap than an alpine spur. But in winter, when the snow is down into the valleys, it is at once majestic and magical, like everyone's dream of Switzerland, or a memory of European Christmases.

Lake Tekapo, Mackenzie Country. (above)
A true alpine lake, Lake Tekapo was once
an ancient glacier, a prehistoric ice-burden
which the surrounding countryside has
never quite forgotten or forgiven. Near the
lake's verge, the feathery snowgrass,
foxglove and the spiny matagouri seem to
be all that is willing to inhabit the thin
soil covering the ancient moraine.

Glendhu Bay, Lake Wanaka. (right)
Though the autumn days are warm, the
shingly beach of Glendhu Bay is deserted
by evening, when the last rays of the
lowering sun are defeated by the early
evening chill, and the cold comes creeping
across the deep waters of Lake Wanaka
which, it is suddenly easy to recall, was
once a mass of glacier ice, thousands of
metres thick.

near-desert, areas of immoderately high rainfall and lush forest of almost
sub-tropical luxuriance, areas which experience each winter a heavy and
sustained snowfall, areas of crackling frosts, and areas with an enviable tally
of annual sunshine hours.

The moisture-laden winds from the Tasman Sea bring clouds which are
literally trapped on the western side of the Southern Alps, and are forced to
such altitudes that they precipitate heavily on the narrow coastal strip on the
mountains' western side. The north-west winds, buffeting their way
through mountain valleys as through gigantic wind-tunnels, burst upon the
eastern plains with great and sometimes destructive force.

The eternal snows upon those prodigious peaks refrigerate the winter air,
so that east-coast towns, cities and farmlands receive a disinfecting poultice
of frost on clear nights from late March till late September.

No South Islander lives more than two or three hours' drive from ski-
slopes, ice-bound skating ponds and lakes and snowy hillsides from July to
October. Few have not at least a nodding acquaintance with the high
country, and some memorable experiences of the great ranges, or at least of
some memorable mountain mood or spectacle, such as the first rays of the
morning sun touching Mount Cook's summit with flame while the land is
still dark with night, or the last pink glow of the setting sun, or the reflected
mirror-brightness of the moonlight on the snow-clad face of the
Remarkables, or the snow-covered peaks of the Kaikouras seeming to lean
over the calm bay. No matter where South Islanders live — on the broad,
billiard-table-flat plains of Canterbury, or the rolling hills of North Otago,
or the rock-bound Kaikoura coast, or in the high upland basins of Amuri or
the Mackenzie Country, or the rock-ribbed, glacier-planed terraces of Central
Otago, or in the bustling towns and cities — every South Islander is, in some
special way, a child of the mountains.

Mount Talbot, Fiordland. (above left)

As you drive across Lyttles Flat, where the Homer Tunnel construction village once stood, and which is now hutless, and fragrant with fern and mountain gentian, Mount Talbot, 2,225m (7,300ft), stands before you, its twisted peak retaining pockets of snow all year round. Part of the Barrier Range, a spur of the Darran Mountain complex, the forbidding peak leans back from huge fans of avalanche rock.

Ailsa Mountains, Hollyford Valley, Fiordland. (below left)

From where the Milford Road runs through the Hollyford Valley, the Ailsa Mountains, (right), trend away south-eastward, walling off that jungle-like, beautiful wilderness from the Upper Greenstone Valley. Some of the finest tramping trails in the world wander through these primeval fastnesses.

Glendhu Bay, Lake Wanaka: (right)

A pleasant curve of beach, lined with willow and pine and adding a touch of gentleness to the bulbous, rocky faces of Glendhu Bluff and the stern mountain surroundings, Glendhu Bay is popular with swimmers, in the burning summer heat. In autumn it becomes a favourite haunt of anglers, fishing for brown and rainbow trout and Atlantic salmon.

Lake Ianthe, Westland. (below)

Set in a scenic reserve about 15km from Harihari, this delightful little gem of a lake was named, it is said, by a surveyor-explorer who admired Byron's "Childe Harold's Pilgrimage," which was dedicated to a little girl named Ianthe. If that seems to be a roundabout way of arriving at a name, perhaps the little (5.6 square kilometres) water's very smallness, and the fact that exquisite beauty in so compact a package, by its very contrast with the grandeur of the mountains, brought to mind simple and intimate and charming things.

Bowen Falls, Milford Sound. (above)

Bowen Falls issue from a hanging valley high above the head of Milford Sound. The water plunges, first, onto an inclined, hollowed rock "springboard," from which it leaps out again in a sparkling white arc, to fall into a spray-clouded basin. The leap is most dramatic after rain; but even when the water is draped over the rocky faces of the gash in the forested mountain wall, it is hardly less beautiful.

Clinton Canyon, Milford Track. (far left)

Part of the famous Milford Track winds beside the Clinton River for 23km (14 miles)through the mountain-walled valley known as the Clinton Canyon. The forested mountains rise straight up from the valley floor for perhaps 1,200m (4,000ft), then lean back as they stab skyward with spear-point peaks to some 1,830m (6,000ft) above sea level. The canyon climbs, eventually, to Mackinnon Pass, reaching up through moss-hung, twisted mountain beeches to an open area of ranunculus and mountain daisy, where *keas* come close, unafraid and friendly.

15

Fox Glacier. (left)

Fox Glacier's somewhat zig-zagging course brings the great ice-river down from the neve, the vast, eternal snowfields in their inclined basin between the Fritz and Fox Ranges, to a landscape of spurs covered with forest of almost tropical luxuriance.From the glacier's terminal face issues the Fox River, bursting out from an ice cave,carrying great chunks of ice as it hurries down to join the Cook River.

The Okuru River and South Westland Mountains. (above)

From Okuru, south of Haast, the great forested humps of hill stand up above bush and swamp to form outriders of Mount Aspiring National Park, southern extremity of the Alps proper. This is untouched country — the snow-fed river, swelled by many a tributary creek, sliding across the coastal flats, flanked by sedges and flax, with a backing of shrubs, which in turn give way to tall forest trees.

High Country Road near Glenmore Station, Mackenzie Country. (above)

Towards the head of Lake Tekapo, in the brown snowgrass-and-tussock landscape of the Mackenzie Country with its shelter belts of dark, hardy pine, the Godley Peaks rise up, snow-covered in winter, but in summer eroded and barren, like gigantic heaps of gravel, crumbling slowly to choke the Canterbury rivers and build up the vast gravel flats of the Mackenzie Basin.

Shotover River at Arthurs Point, Central Otago. (right)

All the fascinating contradictions of the Central Otago landscape, (right), show in the Shotover River's writhing valley, near Queenstown. Here are the typical rock-ribbed hills, furred with brown, sun-scorched grasses and patched with matagouri and tough briars. Here are the poplars and willows, autumn-yellow as the first frosts paint them; and amidst the harshness there is, here and there, the lush green of a cultivated field. But always, winding across the scene, are the Central Otago rivers, depositing their frequently gold-bearing gravels at the feet of rocky, broom-cladspurs.

Lake Te Anau. (above)

Biggest of the South Island's lakes is Te Anau, its western shores towered over by the densely forested Murchison Mountains, its eastern side gentle with willow and bluegum where an easy, rolling countryside comes down to its shore. In the dark mountains, in 1948, two fascinating discoveries were made. By a small tarn, high in the mountains, tracks led to the finding of a bird long thought to be extinct, the colourful *takahe;* and near the lake's shore, almost directly beneath the tarn, the legendary and long forgotten Te Ana-Au Caves were uncovered, with their glow-worm displays rivalling those of Waitomo.

Lake Quill and Sutherland Falls. (right)

Cupped in the mountains of the Milford Sound district, Lake Quill pours a steady stream of water from a jug-like lip, to form Sutherland Falls, highest in New Zealand and third highest in the world. The first leap of the falls is a lofty 288m (815ft), the second 229m (751ft) and the third 103m (338ft). The Sutherland Falls are one of the principal attractions along the world-famed Milford Track. When Lake Quill is in flood, the Sutherland Falls curve out in a single, spectacular leap of 1,904ft.

Lakes Tekapo and Alexandrina, from Mount John: (above)

The Mackenzie Country lakes are of two kinds — snow-fed and rain-fed. Snow-fed lakes, like Tekapo, are a beautiful lapis-lazuli blue, and rain-water lakes, like Alexandrina, are green-glass clear. The Mackenzie Basin, a region named after the Scottish Highland shepherd who discovered it, (and tried to stock it with stolen sheep), is a wild expanse of tussock and snowgrass and clear mountain air. On Mount John has been set an observatory, to take advantage of the clear, dry atmosphere.

21

Mount Tasman, from Fox, South Westland (below)

The peaks of the Southern Alps are never more spectacular, never more clearly, magnificently displayed, than they are from South Westland, that narrow coastal shelf at their very feet. Mount Tasman, 3,498m (11,475ft), cradles on its faces the snows which feed the Balfour and Abel Janzoon Glaciers, the latter spilling down into the vast neve which give birth to the mighty Fox Glacier.

Fox Glacier from Clearwater Flat. (left)

The Clearwater River rattles over stony shallows along the edge of a typical Westland river flat, which it shares with the Cook River. Its waters reflect the almost theatrical spectacle of clouds slowly parting like stage curtains to reveal, first the Fox Glacier in its notch in the granite mountains, and then the splendour of the stupendous peaks from which it flows.

Mount Cook and Sealy Tarn.

Mount Cook, Aorangi, the Cloud-Piercer, New Zealand's highest mountain, with the long chain of peaks trailing southward to form an impressive wall on the eastern side of the Hooker Glacier, is awe-inspiring country. From Sealy Tarn, little can be seen of the Hooker Glacier but the long heaping of gravel and boulders which it has left behind in its retreat back into the high reaches beneath Turner Peak and Proud Pass. But in mountain meadows such as this grow the famed Mount Cook lily, *(Ranunculus Lyellii, upper right)*, and the mountain daisy, *(Celmisia)*, lower right, which, in season, are a sight worth seeing.

Lake Matheson, Westland. (over)

Lake Matheson, near Fox Glacier in South Westland, is a more familiar sight to most New Zealanders and many overseas visitors than far bigger lakes — because the quality of its mountain reflections makes this bush-fringed little water a favourite photographic subject. It was once a huge block of ice, left behind in ancient times by the receding glacier, and the forest which crowds down to its brim grows over a moraine which was left behind, marking a stage in the glacier's early growth, before it began its long retreat.

Westland Bush and Stream (left)

On the western side of the ranges, where the rainfall is frequent and heavy, the bush has an almost tropical luxuriance. Living trees are coated, furred, festooned with parasitic growth. Dead forest giants lie on the forest floor, crumbling beneath a burden of fungi and mosses. An unbelievable variety of ferns peers from flying-buttress root systems of trees, or reach for the sky on rough, palm-like trunks. Strange and riotous growth clothes mossy banks and droops from host trees; and the whole struggling growth fights upward, competing for a share of sunshine.

Lake Brunner from Lone Tree Lookout, Westland. (below)

When they found it in its high setting of forested foothills, Europeans named it Lake Brunner. The Maori, perhaps more alive to the poetry of its calm beauty, had long before named it *Moana Kotuku*, the Sea of the White Heron. Whatever it is called, this beautiful water is just that, a vista of calm loveliness spreading across 26 square kilometres, (16 square miles), largest of all the Westland lakes. It is constantly replenished by the runoff of Westland's heavy and frequent rains in the surrounding mountains.

Sheep Mustering Beneath Mount Cook, Mackenzie Country. (over above)

In the Canterbury high country, merino sheep graze all through summer on the sparse, sun-ripened grasses, foraging over the tops of hills which, in another country would be listed among the high mountains. But always, snow-covered Mount Cook and the central massif of the Southern Alps gaze down upon the dun-coloured pastures, and chill with their snows the breath of the westerly winds, even in high summer.

Mount Aspiring, Southern Alps. (far right)

The great spire of Mount Aspiring soars 3,135m (9,957ft), into the sky, towering above the surrounding peaks of Stargazer, Mt Joffre, Mt French, Moonraker, MtAvalanche — a great white fang of a peak after which is named the Mount Aspiring National Park, a wilderness of eternally snow-covered tops and deep, densely forested valleys spreading over an immense 287,205ha.

Ski-Plane on Tasman Glacier. (right)

The Tasman Glacier, sweeping down like a gleaming 29km (18-mile) staircase from beneath the 3,109m (10,200ft) peak of Mt Elie de Beaumont to the gravelly valley of the Tasman River, may be climbed. But it is more easily, more spectacularly mounted in a ski-plane, which flies its passengers around the mighty peaks, and lands you on the glacier's neve, a matchlessly thrilling experience.

The Lighthouse, Skippers Road, Queenstown. (above)

The famous — or infamous — road that wanders and climbs precariously through Skippers Canyon leads into a harsh landscape, where the rocky frame of the mountains bursts out through the thin, parched soil, and rock, formations have inspired fanciful names, like the Lighthouse, (above.) Perhaps the gold-fossickers found it comforting, in this unforgiving land, to imagine that such features might have been raised by men's hands rather than rudely sculpted, as they were, by climatic severity.

Remarkables Landscape, near Queenstown. (above right)

As if relenting briefly, Central Otago now and again smiles in scenes of pastoral peace, (right, above), such as these green and pleasant fields at the foot of the stern Remarkables Range — pockets of sun-trapped fertility amid the rugged mountains. The Remarkables, with peaks over 2,100m (7,000ft) high, and harsh, seamed faces, loom over Lake Wakatipu and make the soft pastures seem even more gentle by comparison. But even in these grassy fields, the hardy Merino and Corriedale do best, thriving where other breeds would succumb to the fierce alpine climate.

Lake Alexandrina, Mackenzie Country. (below right)

Lake Alexandrina, (right), close to Lake Tekapo, forms a soft and comfortable oasis in the quilted landscape of brown hills. Even the water looks different from that of its neighbour, for this lake is rain-fed, not snow-fed. From the air, the contrasting colours of the snow-fed and rain-fed lakes of the Mackenzie Basin give an impression of jewels in a golden setting.

Skippers Bridge and the Upper Shotover River. (above)

Into the dark and forbidding mountain country, in the 1860s, came thousands of gold-seekers; and the Shotover River, (above), rewarded many of them richly. From others it witheld its wealth, and yet others it drowned, trapping them in its sudden floods, in deep and rocky gorges. In this kind of country man's engineering appears frail and spidery beside the superlative landscape of rock and crag.

Frankton Arm, Lake Wakatipu, and the Remarkables. (left)

The Frankton Arm of Lake Wakatipu pokes eastward from the main body of the lake, running beneath the rugged faces of the Remarkables Range, lapping the geometrically square shore of the peninsula at Queenstown, and the pine-covered tip of Kelvin Heights peninsula. The township of Frankton spreads itself down to the water's edge, where the lake waters gather for a turbulent rush through the Kawarau Gorge.

Tasman Glacier Skifield, Southern Alps. (above)

The Tasman Glacier skifield is not, as one might think, a fast, downhill 29km run, but rather something of a ski-travelling journey over slopes of varying steepness, traversing flats and mounds, for a distance of about 8km. It is principally a wonderful wander amongst magnificent alpine scenery — but the guides recommend it only for experienced skiers.

Hooker Glacier, Southern Alps. (right)

The Empress, Noeline and Mona Glacier, pushing down from Endeavour Col on the Mount Cook Range, are brought up short by the high wall of rock where the Baker Saddle climbs between La Perouse and the lesser Dilemma Peak. Not to be denied, they swing southward, combining into one great ice-fall, the Hooker Glacier, comparatively short, steep and spectacular.

Tui Tarn, Cass River, Mackenzie Country. (left)

There are two Cass Rivers in Canterbury — but to trampers of the bare, almost sub-antarctic upland of the Mackenzie, the best-known Cass River is the one which runs down from a high valley between the Liebig and Hall Ranges to Lake Tekapo. Though its domain is bare and windswept, it possesses the lonely, wild glory reflected in the still, cold waters of Tui Tarn.

Lake Ohau, Mackenzie Country. (below right)

Like other lakes of glacial origin, Ohau is surrounded by superb mountain scenery, the high, snow-covered ranges rising from the water's edge; and close to the tourist lodge, which sits on this broad shelf overlooking the lake, is a fine skifield. Ohau is the southernmost of the Mackenzie Country lakes, and perhaps the most spectacular, being more like the alpine lakes of Central Otago than are Tekapo, Pukaki or Alexandrina. At an altitude of 524m (1,720ft), Ohau spreads over 23 square miles.

Lindis Pass Hills. (right)

The Lindis Pass, where a narrow, dusty road slips through from the Mackenzie Basin to Central Otago, is a place of snow and floods in winter, and of oven-like heat in summer, when the hills are baked, brown and resemble the folds of a carelessly dropped blanket. The Lindis Pass was known to the old-time Maoris, who wandered frequently over its 1,006m (3,300ft) altitude.

Purakaunui Falls, South Otago. (over page)

Purakaunui Falls, in the Catlins District of South Otago, is an exquisitely set cascade in a tract of native forest, on steeply falling land near the coast. Easily reached by a walkway from the road, the falls are rapidly becoming a premier tourist attraction. (Though the setting is beautiful, the name has unpleasant associations. It means "Big Stack of Firewood," and is a contemptuous reference to the bodies of Maori warriors slain in one of their olden tribal battles, and stacked ready for cooking and eating.)

Lake Hawea, Otago.

Lake Hawea, lying in the bed of a
prehistoric glacier, is some 48 square miles
in area — 35km (22 miles) long, and up to
8km (5 miles) wide. Magnificently
overlooked by the range which runs
between Mount Grandview and Dingle
Peak, the lake has that frequently found
quality of mirror stillness which seems to
be characteristic of lakes of glacial origin;
and when the dusk gathers early, as it does
in such deep mountain valleys, the high,
still-daylit clouds are reflected perfectly in
the glassy water, giving back a second-
hand light which holds back the darkness
on the valley floor for a little while
longer.

Tree Fern Fronds.

In the Westland rain forests, at the feet of
the high Alps, on that narrow shelf
between the mountains and the sea, the
tree ferns, (right), grow to prodigious size,
their budding, violin-neck fronds opening
out, palm-tree-like, to sway and wave
along the roadsides at the edge of the dark
bush. Such fronds were a frequent element
in the art of the Maori carver.

Buller River at Lake Rotoroa, Nelson Lakes District. (top left)

Where the main alpine chain frays out at its northern end into a fantastic tangle of complicated ranges, in a region criss-crossed with deep rift valleys, lie Lakes Rotoiti and Rotoroa, set like jewels in the forested mountains; and from Lake Rotoroa, the larger of the two, issues the Buller River, lusty and powerful and deep, right from its source and all the way down to the Tasman Sea.

Upper Waimakariri, Canterbury. (above)

The upper reaches of the Waimakariri (Cold Waters) River, where it wanders out from the high alps, are a tangled skein of gravel-choked waterways, subject to sudden floods, (which, in a more populous area, would be massively destructive), when the snows melt or there

are heavy rains in the mountain valleys. The Waimakariri, like the Rangitata and the Rakaia, waters the broad Canterbury Plain, which, indeed, these mountain-bred rivers helped to form, by bringing gravels down from the mountainsides and depositing them in the shallow sea which once washed the skirts of the foothills.

Upper Wairau River, Marlborough. (below left)

The Wairau River begins in a long fold in that crumpled country east of the Spenser Mountains. It tumbles down through high-altitude beech forests into a fen and tussock basin beneath Mount Alma, and swings sharply northward, to brawl and foam beneath the eastern faces of the St Arnaud Range, in a forest-filled valley, as it flows on its way to the Pacific Ocean.

Lake Marian and Mount Crosscut. (left)
Tucked into the folds of the mountains, at the head of the Marian Valley in the Hollyford region of Fiordland, Lake Marian lies below the Lyttle Falls, which leap down from a hanging valley holding two more small lakes. In this valley, which runs east-west between the precipitous and imposing faces of Mount Christine and Mount Crosscut — in this almost overpowering area — a Surveyor-General, E.H.Wilmot, chose to bestow the name of a young cousin. Not only did he name the valley after her, but also the sublime little lake, plus two lakes near the head of the falls, which he named Mariana and Marianette, a dainty nomenclature for such a powerful landscape.

Craigieburn Skifield. (above)
On the road that leads from Christchurch to Arthurs Pass, there are some four fine skifields, mostly operated by ski clubs — family fields, a mere hour and a half by car from Christchurch. The Craigieburn field has a rope tow and other essential facilities; nothing large or opulent, but enough to ensure skiers of all levels of skills, competitive skiers, fun skiers and complete tyros, a good day's fun for a good price. On the slopes in this area, the Forestry Department has been conducting a trial planting of pines, which will serve to hold together slopes which, when not under snow, erode massively.

THE HAND OF MAN.

Even surrounded by a superabundance of natural beauty, man still has other needs. He might not live by bread alone, but bread he must have to live at all. So he drills and marshalls his landscape until it functions like his own machinery, to feed and clothe and house him. Also, though there are a few exceptional people for whom the untamed wilderness is all they need, there are many more for whom the wild beauty is better taken in small sips. The mass of people, though they enjoy the grandeur of mountains and the riotous growth of the bush, have a need for ordered paths, barbered lawns and disciplined, flowery gardens.

In addition, those brave souls who first abondoned their familiar English scene to settle in a new and alien land experienced a crushing homesickness. To aleviate its very real pain, they hastened to establish in their new soil the style of buildings, even the trees, flowers, animals and birds they had known and loved in the Old Country.

Yet it could never be a real duplication. For one thing, there was so much more land to spare. Farms were measured in thousands of acres, sheep runs in hundreds of square miles, rather than the neat, small, intensely cultivated holdings of rural England, measured in fifties or hundreds of acres. Every householder was encouraged to build his home on a half-acre or quarter-acre section, with the result that populations which would have fitted easily into a small cluster of semi-detached cottages bordering a quarter of a mile of English road, here sprawled over a square mile of perfectly farmable landscape; and the larger centres sprawled outward over areas that would have contained an English city.

Even architecture could not entirely reproduce the familiar English scene. The traditional methods of building were not entirely suitable. Nogging, for example, that style of building which is usually labelled "Tudor," though it is much older than that, consisting of an exposed framing with the bricks laid in between the frame members, proved unsatisfactory in New Zealand because of the ferocious shrinkage coefficient of New Zealand timbers. The ancient stone houses and ecclesiastical buildings which, in England, had stood for centuries had not had to cope with the not infrequent earthquakes in this geologically younger land.

So architecture and building practices became a sort of compromise, out of which has grown some original and striking innovations.

Some native trees did provide some exceptionally fine building timbers; but the best of such timbers were slow-growing; and, moreover, early

Lily Gigantum, Mount Peel Homestead Grounds, Canterbury.
Old World trees and Old World wildflowers create an English woodland of stately oak and trumpets of Lily Gigantum in country which must have seemed, to the first Mount Peel settlers, to be a dreary, alien, tussock-covered wilderness at the feet of the overbearing mountains.

The Christchurch Town Hall and Ferrier Fountain. (above)

On the banks of the principal stream, the Pilgrims' descendents built their Town Hall complex, purely New Zealand in its architecture, yet somehow as English as a medieval castle. And in its courtyard, to offset its severity, they set fountains like giant thistledown.

Daffodils, Botanical Gardens, Christchurch. (right)

On a swampy site, in heavy soil laced with a network of peaty streams, the Canterbury Pilgrims built a city. In its midst, they reserved 497 acres of hard-won ground, to serve as a park and a garden, so that city dwellers would never lack for out-door spaces; and in the middle of the park, they planted a garden of English trees, and patched the greensward with beds of daffodils, so that spring in the heart of Christchurch would always remind them of April in England . . .

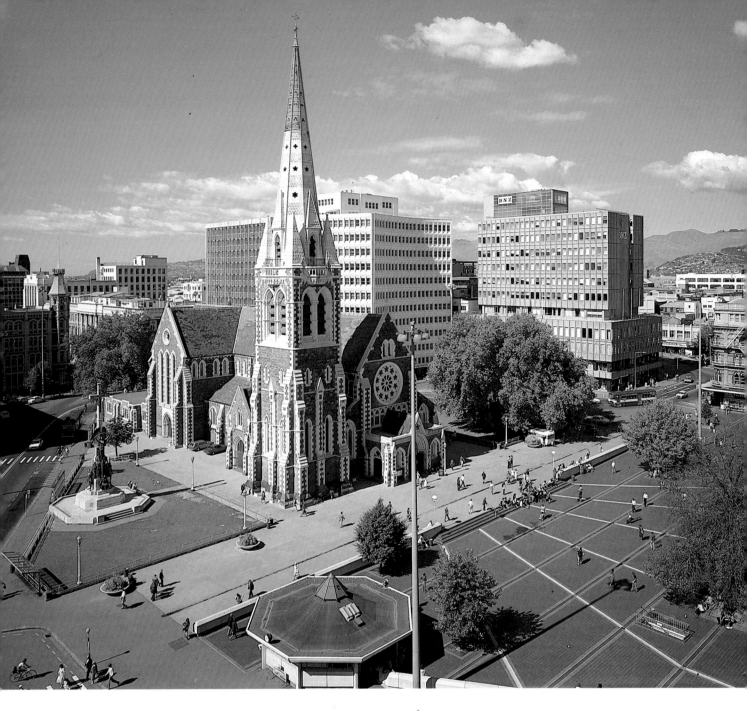

Christchurch Cathedral, and Cathedral Square. (above)

At the city's heart, they raised a Gothic cathedral, to denote the nature of their settlement and the direction of their own ideals. For the Canterbury Pilgrims were principally a Church of England band, and the Church originally undertook their pastoral and educational care. It was planned from the first that Christchurch should have a public school, (English style), and a University; and the University Chapel was to double as a Cathedral. Circumstances changed these schemes somewhat, but the Cathedral was built where originally the school and university were to have stood — in the centre of the city.

exploitation brought at least one species to the verge of extinction. Certain exotic trees, notably the radiata pine, were found to grow rapidly and well — so over the past fifty years, vast areas have been planted, hundreds of square miles of geometrically rectangular stands, tidily, rigidly separated into dark green regiments by access road and fire-break.

The rivers which flow mightily down to the ocean from upland lake and permanent snowfield have proved to be eminently harnessable for the production of electric power, or the irrigation of otherwise waste areas, or both. This has not infrequently resulted in the creation of vast lakes, with resultant change of local weather patterns over certain areas.

51

The Canterbury Plains. (left)
The patchwork that is the Canterbury
Plains is created by an heroic amount of
sheer hard work — meticulously straight
fencelines, the careful rotating of crop and
pasture, and the dark lines of pine and
macrocarpa windbreaks, planted to protect
the light, silty topsoil from the boisterous
nor'west winds.

Timaru Harbour and Wharves. (above)
The prodigious nineteenth century
engineering, with horse and dray and
wheelbarrow and pick and shovel, steam-
winches and primitive explosives, that
created a port out a shallow indentation
in Canterbury's Pacific coast now provides
an outlet point for the abundant produce
of richly alluvial plains and the fertile,
rolling hills of hinterland. Lyttelton, on
Banks Peninsula, was always the principal
Canterbury port; but in the days before the
treacherous Rakaia and Rangitata Rivers
were adequately bridged, men had to find
another means of exporting seasonal
produce. Timaru therefore became
established as a port, and prospered.

Otago Peninsula. (over page)
An echo of old Scotland is in the dry-stone fences, the sheltering clumps of wind-sculpted trees, the occasional blaze of gorse and the tidy houses and barns, where Otago Peninsula lies alongside a harbour which is like a long and narrow loch. A mere stone's throw from the city of Dunedin, the peninsula is considered to be in it, but is not really of it, being a different world entirely from the busy city across the harbour.

Tobacco Harvesting, Motueka Valley, Nelson. (above)
In Nelson Province, which is northerly enough to ensure mild winters, the spurs of the ranges enclose the fertile Motueka Valley, making it a sheltered sun-trap which yields fine harvests of tobacco, (above), along with hops and fruit, which is harvested at the end of the district's long growing season. Few New Zealanders are fully aware of the ideal climate in this region. Although it is indeed in the South Island, it lies on a latitude not far removed from that of the Hawkes Bay fruitbowl; and with high ranges giving protection from the Tasman Seaboard weather, it enjoys an east coast climate.

Nelson, from Quebec Road. (above right)
Nelson nestles about the curve of its bay, with hills rising steeply at its back — a

thriving centre for the richly fertile valleys in the folds of the northern ranges.
Once— and perhaps still — a favourite retirement spot because of its gently warm climate, it is today a thriving and busy city, surrounded by an intriguing mix of modern industrial complexes and cottage industries.

Pine Forest, Whangamoa, Nelson. (below right)
Vast acreages of pine, regimentally aligned, clothe the slopes of the high hills of Nelson province, (right), providing timber and, incidentally, holding firmly together slopes which would otherwise erode massively. Pine chips from the region have become a significant export, contributing handsomely to the whole country's economy.

Alpine Night, Queenstown and Lake Wakatipu. (previous page left)

There are lights to twinkle across the Frankton Arm of Lake Wakatipu when the daylight fails and the frost chills the evening air in Queenstown, (above.) In Queenstown itself, for most of the year, are heard the languages and accents of almost every country in the world, as tourists flock here for the summer and autumn sightseeing, and in winter and early spring for the magnificent skiing.

Main Street, Arrowtown. (previous page below)

When autumn colours the avenue in Arrowtown, the cosy cottages built by the old gold-seekers of last century come into their own, being small, for easy heating, and touchingly home-like, the kind of cottages that everyone's Granny lived in.

The town was built by goldminers in the 'sixties of last century, and has altered little since then. Even the newer houses and holiday homes hereabouts seek out the sunny slopes and sheltered nooks of this snug shelf at the foot of the high ranges. The first-comers won more than 200lb (100kg) of gold in the first few weeks, in this vicinity.

Old Coaching Inn, Skippers Road, Queenstown. (previous page above)

The old inn remembers the days when the modern twenty-minute drive over good roads between Queenstown and Arrowtown was an arduous, punishing day's travel by pack-train or, later, two or three hours' journey by coach.

Queenstown, Lake Wakatipu and Walter Peak. (above left)

Lovely Queenstown is a garden built and flourishing upon what was once a tumble of rock, the terminal moraine of a glacier. A colourful town with a colourful past, it clusters down to its little, square bay and its miniature wharves as its former inhabitants used to do, as though still welcoming boatloads of gold prospectors arriving from Kingston, at the lake's southern end.

Arrow Basin, near Queenstown. (above)

Even the killing frosts of winter and the broiling suns of summer have not been able to prevent men from planting and cultivating and creating soft oases in the hard Arrow Basin country. As the gold-seekers crowded into these wild mountain valleys, farmers also came — not to gamble on finding fortunes in gold, but settling for the certainty that the miners would need food, and that farmers and farms would still be needed when all the gold had gone.

Otago Peninsula Rural Scene. (left)

The afternoon sun that touches the old volcanic rim of Otago Peninsula lights a scene of pastoral peace, where farms are spread and sheep graze about the ancient, towering lava plugs; for, like Lyttelton to the north, Otago Harbour is a drowned volcanic crater, in which ancient lava spillings form reefs along its eastern shore. The peninsula is almost parallel to the mainland shore, forming the eastern wall of a long, narrow harbour with one winding, dredged, deep-water channel which was contrived to bring ships to the commercial heart of Dunedin.

Dunedin Sunrise. (below)

The early morning sun gilds the city of Dunedin, built like Rome upon its seven hills, across the harbour from the Peninsula. The sun's first rays touch the tops of the man-made towers, the high-rise blocks on the university campus at the northern end of the town. Otago settlers built their city on land rejected by the Canterbury colonists as being too rough, hilly and densely forested.

Acheron Accommodation House, Marlborough. (above left)

The early settlers found the tussock-covered hills of Marlborough's high country ideal for sheep. But for sheep there had to be shepherds and drovers, and for these there had to be shelter against potential lethal high-country weather. Accommodation houses were built, such as this one at Acheron, near the head of the Clarence River. In this virtually treeless region, it had to be built of the very ground on which it stands, of cob, which is a puddled mixture of clay, chopped tussock and chaff.

Hereford Cattle, Lake Hawea, Otago. (left)

Along the western shore of Lake Hawea, beneath frowning peaks, a broad shelf of land, (left), is a sheltered Shangri-la,

where fine Hereford cattle graze and grow fat. On these "flats," in days gone by, cereal crops have been grown, of such fine quality that buyers were attracted from all over the country.

Sheep, Lake Johnson, Otago. (above)

Near Lake Johnson, (above), sheep thrive in a similar green and unexpected oasis. Lake Johnson is a small lake near Lake Hayes, in the Wakatipu Region. Its principal claim to fame is the fine trout fishing it affords, both brown and rainbow trout being caught in its still and sheltered waters. The lake's surroundings are not in the least typical of the rugged Central Otago landscape, being rolling green downs, more typical of South Canterbury or coastal Otago.

Benmore Hydro Dam and Lake. (above)
Forty years after Lake Mahinerangi was
formed, in an immensely larger
undertaking, engineers raised an earth
dam between two hills near Otematata,
behind which the Waitaki River backed
up to fill the twisting, deep valleys.
Benmore, (above), is one of the largest
earth dams in the world. It stands 110m
(360ft) high, 1,219m (4,000ft) long. Its lake
covers 8,300ha (32sq miles) with a
hundred miles of shoreline and 17 islands.
Its power output is 540,000kw, over 2,400
million units per year.

Evening Light, Lake Mahinerangi, Otago.
(right)
Where once a simple hill country stream
wriggled down through Waipori Gorge,
south of Dunedin, engineers in the early
years of this century built a dam, forming
an artificial lake to store water for the
Waipori Electric Power Stations. It was
named Mahinerangi, not after some
legendary Maori princess, but after the
daughter of Dunedin's (1911) Mayor.

Molesworth Cattle Drive, Marlborough. (above)

In the Marlborough highlands, on the broad, steep Molesworth Station, a summer cattle muster over the station's 460,000 mountainous acres begins a cattle drive along steep ridges, over wild river flats and down through the high passes to Culverden sale yards, where the mob is held, to be shipped by truck to Christchurch. Once divided into three vast sheep stations, the land was eaten out and burnt over too hard, too frequently. It became infested with rabbits, its hillsides eroded and the whole area seemingly ruined for livestock production. The Government took it over and it was gradually restored and stocked with cattle. Today it carries some 10,000 head, and serves as a research station for high-country farming.

Lake Tekapo Landscape, Mackenzie Country. (right)

The same fierce heat which scorches the Canterbury Plains is unrelieved over much of the Mackenzie Basin because of the sparsity of shade trees. But it ripens vast acreages of hay, to be mown and stored in huge, round bales, against the hungry winter. For at an altitude of over 700m (2,321ft), Lake Tekapo's climatic severity poses special problems in the maintenance of livestock in the cold months.

Sheep Leaving Yards, Canterbury. (above)
Many Canterbury runs were taken up by
Australian graziers, who brought with
them a better knowledge of farming in a
dry, drought-prone country than the
Englishmen possessed. But it was the
Englishmen who contrived to irrigate
some 2½-million acres with water-race
systems run from Canterbury's biggest
rivers, and increased the land's sheep-
carrying capacity dramatically. Today
close to 300,000 bales of wool are
produced annually in this area, and in
some years, over four million prime lamb
carceases are exported — a significant part
of New Zealand's overall earnings.

69

Harvesting, Canterbury Plains. (above left)
The patchwork of the Canterbury Plains is composed of alternating fields of pasture, fodder crops and cereal crops, including barley, oats and wheat, with sowings of winter feed for sheep, all separated by fences which were originally, (in that treeless expanse), raised as walls of sods, on which were planted gorse hedges, stockproof and dense enough to give growing crops some measure of shelter.

South Canterbury Rural Scene. (left)
Where the hills begin to rise towards the mountains, around the edges of the Canterbury Plains, (left), pleasant rural dales, hedged and green and shaded with trees, contrast with the wilder hills beyond. There tends to be a fairly sharp demarcation between the rolling pastures of the lower foothills, and the sudden

heights and bush-clad steeps of the sub-alpine ranges. It is a contrast which dramatically accentuates the ordered neatness of those hills which man has brought under cultivation.

Pastoral Scene Near Waikari, North Canterbury. (above)
Waikari, Hawarden and Culverden are three small communities set in a rolling, upland basin walled about with high ranges. Green and fertile, based on great reefs of limestone, the countryside is ideal for sheep, and the little townships bask in the sunshine of long summers, and are snugly sited and hospitable when the high-altitude winters bring snow and crackling frosts.

THE PACIFIC AND TASMAN SHORES.

There is no particular or mystical quality about the Tasman Sea or the Pacific Ocean that would give a unique character to either of the coasts they have shaped along the flanks of this South Island. Both seas attack the shore with equal ferocity, or roll up to it in precisely the same kind of long swell, with a mighty threatening of surf where the continental shelf resists the inrushing water, or with a long, swift tidal rip where an off-shore current races around the turn of a headland and gouges an adjacent sweep of shore.

True, the Pacific coast has miles-long stretches of fine, sandy beach — but the Tasman coast has its Punakaiki, almost tropical under the caress of a warm current, with tall and graceful *nikau* palms, and the jungle-like bush coming down to the shore. True, the Tasman coast has its wild and rocky headlands — but the Pacific coast has its Kaikoura coast, with reef-guarded coves and romantically rock-bound capes and stern peninsulas at whose feet the bull kelp swirls and the incoming tides crash against granite cliffs.

It is the land, the magnificent, overpowering, high-reaching land that seems to marshall the sea and command its currents, deciding the shape of its own shores.

It's an ancient warfare, this battle between ocean and island. Here and there are traces of the sea's victory, as at the northern end of the island, where a network of drowned valleys forms the Marlborough Sounds where the defeated landscape has sunk into the water in a gigantic subsidence between Marlborough's seaward ranges and the distant coast of the South Taranaki Bight; or where the ocean has breached the walls of volcanic craters to form the harbours of Lyttelton, Akaroa and Dunedin. Here and there the land has been victorious, as where its rivers, bringing down gravel from the mountains, built up the Canterbury Plain until it reached out and snared the island which became Banks Peninsula.

In places, the coastline runs across the trend of the mountain ranges, to form a rugged shore deeply indented with bays and coves and land-locked havens, or deeply gashed with fiords. Elsewhere, the plains and coastward hills terminate abruptly in high cliffs, at whose base narrow shingle beaches are pounded by ocean rollers along a steeply shelving shore. And where rivers run out between sheltering headlands, beaches have built up —

Sunrise, Lyttelton Harbour.
The early sun, peeping over the rim of the drowned volcanic crater which forms Lyttelton Harbour wakens the small, pleasant, tree-shaded harbourside settlements that cluster about the walls of the ancient crater. Lyttelton Harbour was to have been the site of Canterbury's principal city, and was named in honour of Lord Lyttelton, the Chairman of the Canterbury Association. But the site proved to be too cramped and too short of fresh water, beneath those basalt walls.

73

Mitre Peak, Milford Sound. (previous page)

The massive peaks which wall Milford Sound rise sheer from the cold, clear water to heights of over 1,500m (5,000ft), and it is their prodigious height which makes the Sound seem narrow, though it is actually up to 5km (3 miles) wide.

The Otago Coast North of Taieri Mouth, Otago. (right)

The South Otago coast, north of Taieri Mouth, runs in successive crescents of sandy beach, swept clean by the current which, diverted from its southward course by Otago Peninsula, swings back inshore again at Brighton, until the out thrust hump of hilly land, bulging into the sea from Taieri Mouth, forces it seaward again.

Stewart Island, Viewed from Cosy Nook, Southland. (above)

Cosy Nook, (left), on the southern coast of the South Island, somewhat protected by the guardian rocks and reefs from boisterous Foveaux Strait, offers a view of distant Stewart Island, with its sharply conical Mount Anglem and its darkly forested ranges.

Ernest Island, Stewart Island. (above)
The South Arm of the magnificent Port
Pegasus harbour on the south-eastern side
of the main island is guarded from the
ocean swell by a great hump of land
indented with coves. Some idea may be
obtained of the sudden violence of the seas
in these parts when even on the lee side of
this hump, anchorages have names like
Disappointment Cove and Fright Cove.
On the windward side, it is hardly
suprising to find tiny Ernest Island,
standing in the mouth of a long, deep
inlet, marked on the charts as a 'small
craft retreat.'' But Ernest Island itself is a
peacefully idyllic knob of land, with its
bird-loud bush, and a tree-fringed, curving
bay on its own leeside.

handsome sweeps of sand backed, sometimes, by bush, and sometimes by
dunes, pale blue-green with marram grass and lupins.

There are beaches that stand behind rocky reefs and gaze out across cold,
southern waters towards the far, ice-bound seas of Antarctica, far beyond the
rim of the horizon. There are beaches that are windswept and wild and
strewn with driftwood. There are even beaches that are a rock-hound's
delight, strewn with gemstones deposited by currents which tore them from
frowning volcanic cliffs. There are beaches which sit at a city's feet, tidy, with
barbered lawns behind them and a safe and gentle, sandy-bottomed bay
lapping at them with gentle tides.

The character of the South Island's coastline is infinitely varied,
abounding in inlets and indentations that make it a small-boat navigator's
paradise. Rich in scenic variety, and dotted with natural wonders such as odd
rock formations, blowholes, caves, cruel reefs, and the white smile of long
curves of surf, it is never far from any New Zealander's door — and it is by no
means the least of the South Island's magnificent scenic attractions.

Toko Mouth, South Otago. (below)
The Toko Stream meanders down to a sandy coast through a reedy, scrub-patched fen, to spill into a bay of calm beauty, gently shelving and safe, where South Otago people have built holiday homes to which they bring their children for the long summer holidays. The area contains a special reserve known as Centennial Park, an excellent camping ground. An ocean current which sweeps along this coast maintains a water temperature of around 15.6°C (60°F) all year round.

Coastal Cliffs Near Kaitangata, South Otago. (right)
South of Toko Mouth, the uprising land stands above the Pacific Ocean atop tall cliffs of crumbly-looking conglomerate which, nevertheless, is as hard as concrete, and is seamed, in the vicinity of Kaitangata, with coal. The coast abounds in fish, and several fleets of small fishing boats operate just off shore, and have their anchorages in river mouths and headland-protected bays.

Southland Dawn, Riverton. (previous page)

At the western extremity of the sandy curve of bay between Invercargill's Oreti Beach and the township of Riverton, Howells Point thrusts eastward, a sheltering spearpoint of a headland, making the estuary of the Aparima and Pourakino Rivers a secure anchorage for fishing boats which operate in the stormy waters of Foveaux Strait.

Oamaru Harbour and Cape Wanbrow. (left)

Oamaru Harbour, (right), sheltered from the southerly winds by Cape Wanbrow, was once a busy coastal port. With the decline of coastal shipping, it has become a haven for a fishing fleet. The harbour — and the town — occupy yet another ancient volcanic crater.

Karitane Coast, Otago. (right)

The Karitane Coast must be one of the most idyllic spots in New Zealand, with its curving, sandy, gently shelving beaches and its romantic peninusula, all backed by a story-book countryside of tidy, green farms. Here, too, small boats form an off-shore fishing fleet, anchoring, between fishing sweeps, in the shelter of the peninsula.

The Moeraki Boulders, North Otago. (left)

Moeraki Beach, on North Otago's coast, is strewn with round septarian stones, geological oddities which seem to have formed around a crystalline centre over aeons of time, much as a pearl forms around a piece of grit in an oyster shell. In Maori lore, the stones are sweet potatoes and gourds, the cargo of a wrecked ancestral canoe.

Punakaiki Seascape. (above)
The Tasman Sea coast can be wild, lonely
and magnificently moody. The beach
south of Punakaiki and north of
Greymouth, (above), with its foaming
breakers and its salt-laden haze is typical
of much of the South Island's west coast
scenery. A warm current just offshore
transforms the coastal hills into a
facsimile of tropical jungle in this area,
even to the fringe of nikau palms that nod
and sway above the beaches.

*Early Morning Scene, East Coast of
Stewart Island. (right)*
Though Stewart Island possesses luxuriant
forests, and coves and sandy beaches that
seem to belong to a tropic isle, it still
manages, in odd places and at certain
times and in certain lights, to convey a
reminder that it is, after all, a last outpost,
the final dot of habitable land, between
the main islands and the Antarctic.

The Pancake Rocks, Punakaiki. (left)
Close to the Porari Rivermouth beach, the same turbulent sea has pounded and gouged and carved a headland into a fantastic semblance of piles of great, grey pancakes, (above.) It is somewhat awe-inspiring, to stand on the ground in this vicinity and feel it tremble to the surge and suck of the sea in long caverns beneath your feet. Here and there, explosions of air compressed at the end of such caverns by the inrushing water have burst through the cavern roofs, forming blowholes through which great geysers of seawater jet high into the air.

Jackson Bay, South Westland. (above right)
Farther south, where the sea reaches almost to the feet of the Alps, its waters seem subdued, lapping gently at the narrow beaches as though overawed at last by the power of the mountains; though even here, storms can send the sea crashing right to the foot of the Jackson Bay cliffs. There is wharfage for coastal vessels here, and the bay has long been a minor port, though of much diminished importance now that roads from the north and the east reach Haast and the cattle runs in this "frontier" area.

Porari Rivermouth, Punakaiki Coast. (below right)
Where the Porari River tumbles down from the hills to the Punakaiki coast, and sweeps out across the sand through a gap in the rugged cliffs, the Tasman Sea has stood back and permitted a fine, sandy beach to establish itself. This part of the west coast is a favourite holiday spot, beautiful, sheltered by seaward-trending, high spurs. Its beaches are gently shelving and safe.

Tahunanui Beach, Nelson. (left)

Throughout Nelson's long, hot summers, Tahunanui Beach, (left), on the shores of Tasman Bay, is crowded with sunloving humanity; but as evening closes in, the oyster catchers and stilts and gulls reassert their ancient ownership as they feed in the wake of a receding tide.

Tarakohe Coast,
Golden Bay, Nelson. (above)

The marble hills of Takaka slope down to the Tarakohe coast on the eastern shores of Golden Bay, that rocky and often spectacular seaboard. Abel Tasman, in 1642, called it "Murderers' Bay," because Maoris attacked his ships' boats while they were on a watering detail, and killed some of his men. Today it is known as Golden Bay, and its climate and deeply indented, attractive coast are well described by such a warm and pleasant title.

Picton, Marlborough Sounds. (above)
It is difficult to realise that Picton, spilling down the slopes from the foot of the bush-clad ranges, is the South Island terminal of the ferry link between the two islands. Once Wellington's rival as proposed seat of Government, the little town (population 3,430) at the head of Queen Charlotte Sound remains a tranquil holiday resort, linked to the workaday south by thin ribbons of road and rail through the protecting hills.

Maori Leap Caves, Kaikoura. (right)
The Maori Leap Caves, (left), near Kaikoura, in limestone cliffs once hammered by the sea, now stand well back from the shore, eerie caverns hung with stalactites dripping like spilled toffee, and hide in their dark corners the ancient bones of seal and penguin amongst the forgotten ocean flotsam of lime-encrusted driftwood and empty shells.

Kaikoura, East coast. (above)

The little town of Kaikoura spreads itself
casually in tiers above a steeply shelving,
shingly beach, its pleasant bay wrapped
protectively in the arms of rocky reef and
stubby peninsula. In the bay, seals fish
alongside men in the long ocean swell;
and over all leans the lofty Seaward
Kaikoura Range, presenting within one
small area a microcosmic view of the
essential South Island — mountain, forest,
farm and shore.

Tennyson Inlet, Marlborough Sounds. (above)

Tennyson Inlet, (above), branching southward from the landlocked waterway known as Tawhitinui Beach, is typical of the Marlborough Sounds — deep, well sheltered and watched over by brown, forest-patched hills, In this network of waterways, a sizeable navy could anchor, but most of the traffic upon these sheltered reaches consists of pleasure boats and the launches which serve otherwise isolated farms.

Okuri Bay & D'Urville Island, Marlborough Sounds. (right)

An ancient and cataclysmic subsidence once plunged a landscape of dovetailing spurs and high ridges deep beneath the waters of the South Taranaki Bight. The hills above Okuri ("Place of Dogs") Bay, (right), and the rugged spurs of D'Urville Island were once the peaks of continuous ranges, now drowned beneath the blue waters of French Pass.

Mt Shewell and Fitzroy Bay, Marlborough Sounds. (left)

Fitzroy Bay, (left), is a complex harbour with many coves and inlets. A long spur from Mount Shewell, 777m (2550ft), runs down to Sheep Point, northern head of the almost landlocked bay, and the hills, and the mountain itself, like most Marlborough Sounds countryside, is a sun-browned pasture grazed over by sheep, and patched with exotic and native forest.

Wharariki Beach, Cape Farewell. (above)

Wharariki Beach, (above) on the western side of Cape Farewell, looks out, past the off-shore rocks, across the stormy Tasman Sea. The region is known for its beautiful sunsets. Cape Farewell was the last land sighted by Captain James Cook as he departed from New Zealand after his first exploratory voyage around the coast, and set sail for Australia.

Kaikoura Coast. (above)

The Kaikoura Ranges run straight, parallel courses to the sea, and drop abruptly into its depths, to form a rugged, rock bound shore of jagged reefs and swirling kelp, (above), south of where the Clarence River pours out from its high, hanging valleys and spreads out across a boulder fan as it rushes down to the sea. Like England's Cornish coast, or the stormy coast of Maine, it is a place of deep little inlets where the crayfish, from which it gets its name, (Kaikoura means "Feast of Crayfish"), are still abundant.

Published in 1982 by
Kowhai Publishing Ltd
59 Cambridge Terrace Christchurch
and 10 Peacock Street Auckland

Illustrations Copyright © Robin Smith Photography Lt
Christchurch
Text Copyright Kowhai Publishing Ltd
Relief map reproduced by permission of the
Department of Lands and Survey.
Cover and title pages designed by Denis Gourley
Layout by Warren Jacobs
Set in Baskerville by Saba Graphics Christchurch
Produced by Hedges & Bell S.E. Asia
Printed and bound in Singapore
ISBN 0 908598 08 4